Full House

Die Namen der 10 abgebildeten Dinge findest du auch im Haus unten.
Streiche die Wörter im Haus mit Farbstift an!

chair radio sofa

bed box

stove clock shelf

table armchair

s	o	f	a			
s	h	e	l	f	s	
c	l	o	c	k	c	t	c
b	t	a	b	l	e	o	h
e	a	b	o	x	t	v	a
d	r	a	d	i	o	e	i
a	r	m	c	h	a	i	r

3 Buchstaben sind übrig geblieben.
Sie ergeben zusammengesetzt den
Namen eines Tieres, das auch in
diesem Haus wohnt. Kannst du es
auf die Tafel zeichnen?

It's a ☐☐☐

Lösung: It's a cat.

The scrambled crossword puzzle

Sortiere die Buchstaben und schreibe die richtigen Wörter in die Kästchen unten.

1. n a k s e
2. o n i l
3. g i t r e
4. e s e h p
5. h e s r o
6. n a l i s
7. n a t
8. t a c

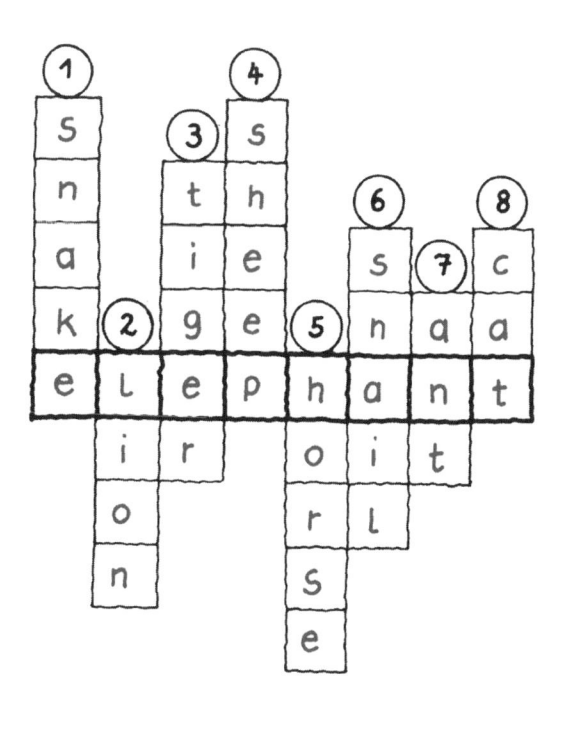

12 months in a year

Trage die jeweiligen Monatsnamen in das Rätselgitter ein!
Beispiel: 6th month (6. Monat) = June

12th month

3rd month

7th month

9th month

6th month

2nd month   d

4th month

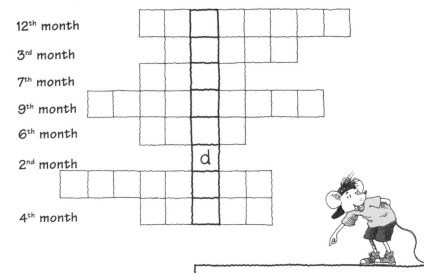

Remember!
The months of the year are proper nouns. They always begin with a capital letter!

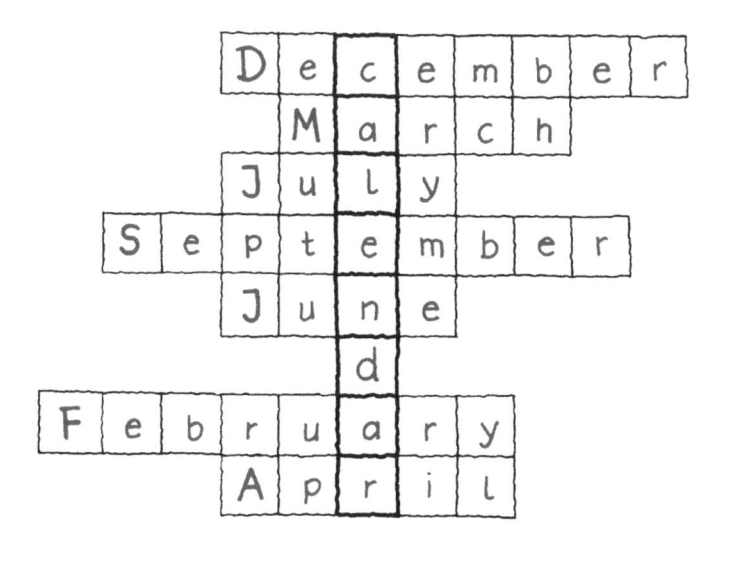

Where are the girls going to?

Linda   Mary   Anne

My name
is Miss Mouse.
What's your name?

the cinema

the town

the zoo

Bilde Sätze!

Anne is going to _____

Mary _____

Linda _____

Anne is going to the cinema.
Mary is going to town.
Linda is going to the zoo.

Clothes

Im Schrank findest du eine Menge Anziehsachen.
Aber Vorsicht! 3 Dinge gehören nicht in den Kleiderschrank.
Streiche sie durch!

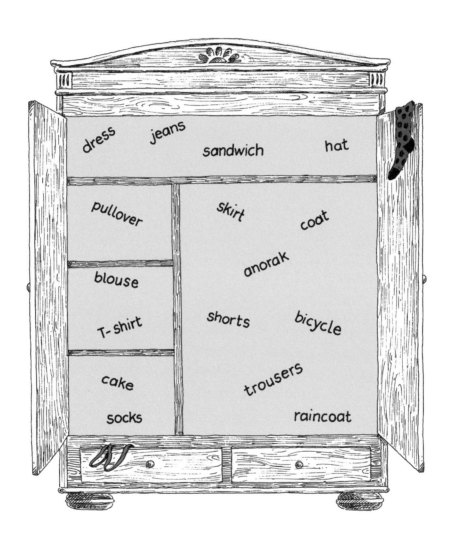

sandwich
cake
bicycle

Clothes

Who is who?

Miss Mouse, Mousey and Mike are good friends.
- Miss Mouse is not the smallest mouse.
- Mousey is not the first in line.
- Mike is smaller than Mousey.

Now, who is who?
Please write their names on the lines!

_____   _____   _____

Miss Mouse – Mousey – Mike

Parts of the body

Verbinde jedes Wort mit dem passenden Körperteil!

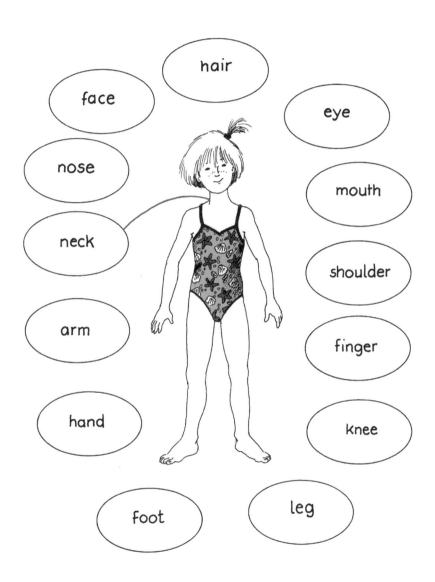

hair

face

eye

nose

mouth

neck

shoulder

arm

finger

hand

knee

foot

leg

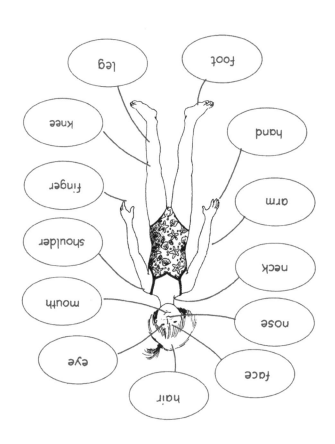

Family

Answer the questions! If you need help, look in the "family-box"!

family-box

uncle   grandfather
aunt father brother
grandmother
sister   mother

How is Mike Grey related to Bill Grey? He is his

How is Kevin White related to Mary Grey? He is her

How is Charles Grey related to Bill Grey? He is his

How is Jane Grey related to Kevin White? She is his

How is Betty Grey related to Charles Grey? She is his

How is Diana Grey related to Bob Grey? She is his

Wenn du die dick umrandeten Buchstaben der Reihe nach hier einträgst, erhältst du den Namen von Baby Grey!

M

Mike Grey is Bill Grey's father.
Kevin White is Mary Grey's uncle.
Charles Grey is Bill Grey's brother.
Jane Grey is Kevin White's sister.
Betty Grey is Charles Grey's mother.
Diana grey is Bob Grey's aunt.

Baby Grey's name is Maureen.

Numbers

Male jedes Kästchen mit einer der folgenden Zahlen aus,
und du erhältst ein Bild!

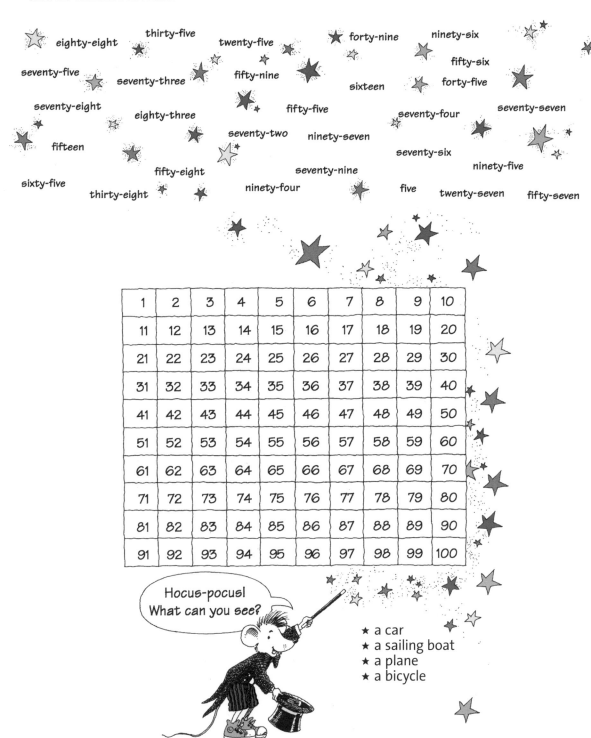

eighty-eight
thirty-five
twenty-five
forty-nine
ninety-six
seventy-five
seventy-three
fifty-nine
fifty-six
sixteen
forty-five
seventy-eight
eighty-three
fifty-five
seventy-four
seventy-seven
fifteen
seventy-two
ninety-seven
seventy-six
sixty-five
fifty-eight
seventy-nine
ninety-five
thirty-eight
ninety-four
five
twenty-seven
fifty-seven

1	2	3	4	5	6	7	8	9	10
11	12	13	14	15	16	17	18	19	20
21	22	23	24	25	26	27	28	29	30
31	32	33	34	35	36	37	38	39	40
41	42	43	44	45	46	47	48	49	50
51	52	53	54	55	56	57	58	59	60
61	62	63	64	65	66	67	68	69	70
71	72	73	74	75	76	77	78	79	80
81	82	83	84	85	86	87	88	89	90
91	92	93	94	95	96	97	98	99	100

Hocus-pocus!
What can you see?

★ a car
★ a sailing boat
★ a plane
★ a bicycle

You can see a sailing boat.

Dinosaurs

Brontosaurus hat 15 Wörter verschluckt, die mit dem Buchstaben „c" beginnen.
Kannst du sie entdecken?

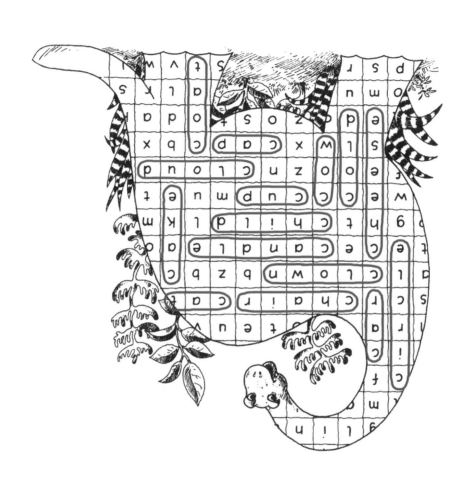

Dinosaurs

Mit den Buchstaben auf Stegosaurus kannst du die Wörter unten
vervollständigen.

Sunday   b_d

r__ler   hor__e

t__ee   _irl

mo__se   b_y

c__r   _able

                chee_e

Sunday
ruler
tree
mouse
car
bed
horse
girl
boy
table
cheese

What does Miss Mouse do?

Suche die Verben im Buchstabengitter, kreise sie ein und schreibe sie
unter die passenden Bilder.

Achtung!
He, she, it, das „s" muss mit!
Schreibe also z. B.: she drinks

Wenn du alles richtig gemacht
hast, bleiben im Gitter 7 Buchstaben übrig. Bilde daraus 2
weitere Verben und schreibe sie
hier neben die deutsche
Bedeutung!

warten – to _____

sehen – to _____

she cries _____   she p___ s___

l	i	s	t	e	n	w	w
a	i	c	l	e	a	n	r
s	l	e	e	p	e	d	i
r	p	l	a	y	a	r	t
e	c	r	y	t	t	e	e
a	d	r	i	v	e	a	r
d	s	f	e	e	d	m	u
t	h	i	n	k	e	e	n

warten – to wait
sehen – to see

l	i	s	t	e	n	w	w
a	i	c	l	e	a	n	r
s	l	e	e	p	e	d	i
r	p	l	a	y	a	r	t
e	c	r	y	t	t	e	e
a	d	r	i	v	e	a	r
d	s	f	e	e	d	m	u
t	h	i	n	k	e	e	n

she writes   she sleeps
she cleans   she eats
she reads   she listens
she thinks   she dreams
she drives   she feeds
she plays   she runs

Opposites

Kennst du das Gegenteil?

stupid   clever

Trage die dick umrandeten Buchstaben der Reihe nach hier ein!

fast – slow	open – closed
sad – happy	cold – hot
right – left	good – bad
last – first	false – true
near – far	light – heavy
over – under	off – on
	long – short
	winter – summer

Lösung: You are a star!

On the farm

Weißt du die Namen der abgebildeten Tiere und Gegenstände?
Sie beginnen alle mit dem Buchstaben „h".

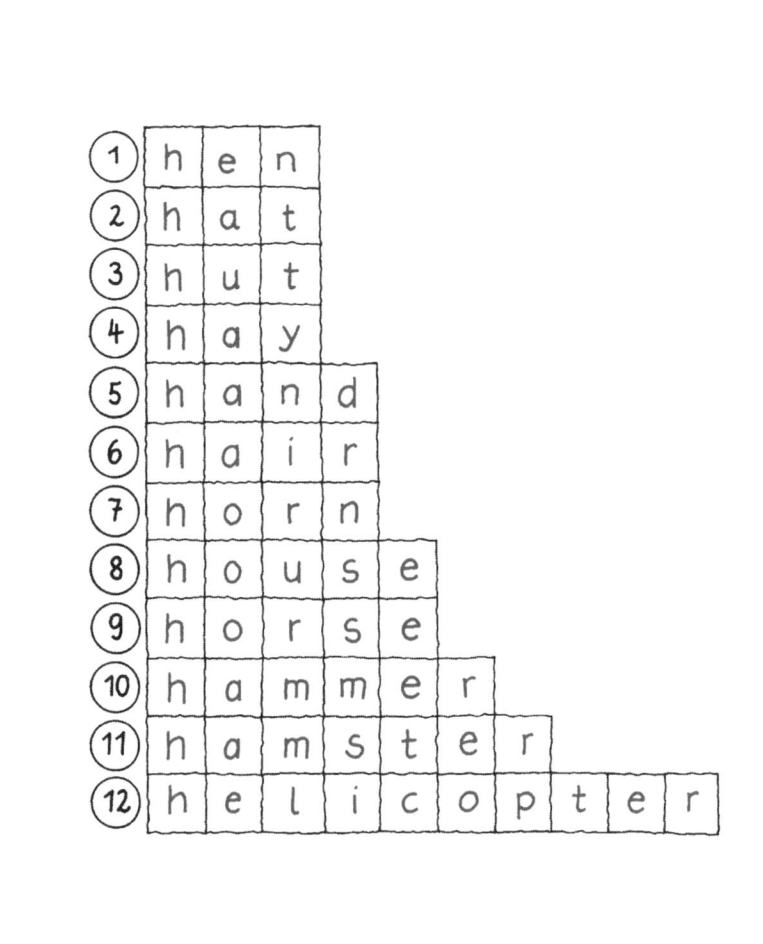

1. h e n
2. h a t
3. h u t
4. h a y
5. h a n d
6. h a i r
7. h o r n
8. h o u s e
9. h o r s e
10. h a m m e r
11. h a m s t e r
12. h e l i c o p t e r

Words with -oo

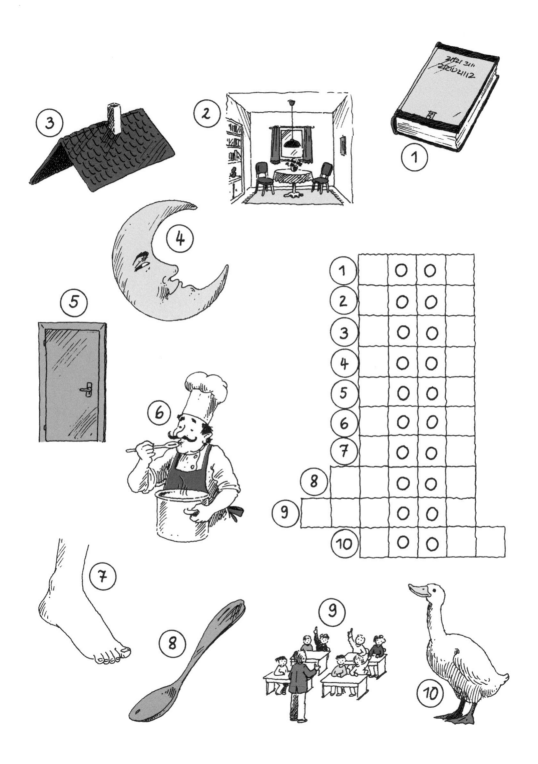

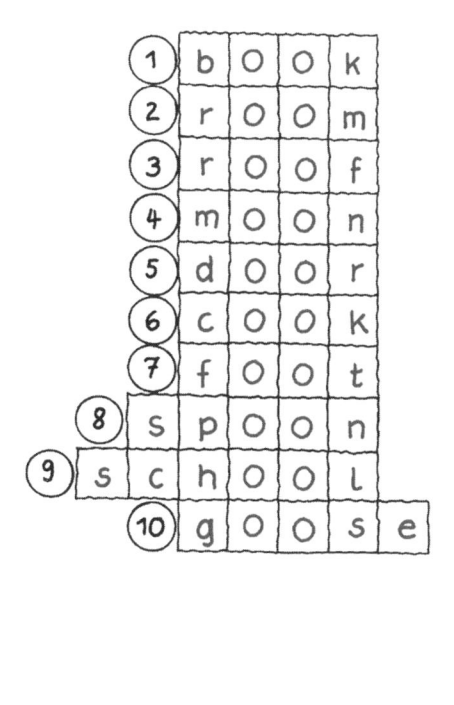

1. b o o k
2. r o o m
3. r o o f
4. m o o n
5. d o o r
6. c o o k
7. f o o t
8. s p o o n
9. s c h o o l
10. g o o s e

Words with -ee

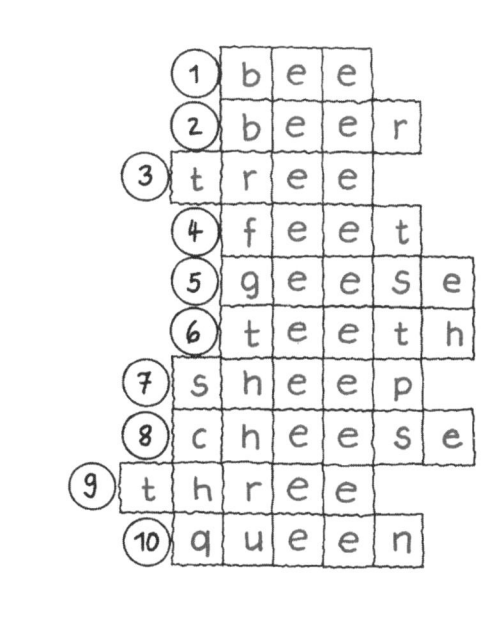

1. bee
2. beer
3. tree
4. feet
5. geese
6. teeth
7. sheep
8. cheese
9. three
10. queen

Horses

Der Bauer ist nicht da. Deshalb soll Sam heute die Pferde in ihre Boxen bringen.
Aber welches Pferd kommt wohin? Kannst du helfen? Verbinde!

Wenn du alles richtig machst, sagen dir die Buchstaben auf
den Pferden, was mit dem Bauern los ist.

Lösung: He is ill.

Tom's room

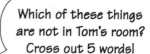

Which of these things are not in Tom's room? Cross out 5 words!

cat   pencil   ball   goose   shoes   poster

radio   lamp   bed   chair   elephant   flag

scissors   satchel   table   trousers   toy car

blanket   apple   window   carpet   glass

plate   T-shirts   train   straw   book

Trage die Anfangsbuchstaben der 5 ausgestrichenen Wörter hier ein!

You are ☐☐☐☐☐ !

Lösung: You are great!

goose
radio
elephant
apple
train

Butterflies

Wenn du die Wörter auf den Flügeln der Schmetterlinge ergänzt und die
hinzugefügten Buchstaben zusammen liest, weißt du, wonach die
Schmetterlinge suchen.

Tipp: Alle 4 Wörter
eines Schmetterlings
beginnen mit demselben
Buchstaben!

The butterflies are looking for ...

fruit	large	elephant
fish	letter	easy
field	lake	egg
fork	lemon	eye

old	window	river
orange	wait	ruler
open	woman	rain
out	watch	run

sweet
some
satchel
snake

Lösung:
The butterflies are
looking for flowers.

Let's rhyme!

Male alle Blasen mit Wörtern, die sich reimen, in derselben Farbe aus!

cat	tree	land
hat	bee	hand
fat	me	sand
rat	she	and

ran		they
pan		grey
man		pay
than		day

At the airport

Die Flugzeuge fliegen zu großen englischen, amerikanischen oder australischen Städten. Ordne die Buchstaben und kreise die 8 richtigen Städte ein!

Atlanta Canberra Washington Manchester Sydney

Bristol Aberdeen Denver London Chicago Adelaide

New York Perth Leeds Dallas Glasgow

The aeroplanes go to:

Washington
Canberra
New York
Sydney
Manchester
London
Chicago
Leeds

Nouns and verbs

Schreibe das passende Verb unter das Bild!

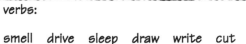

verbs:

smell   drive   sleep   draw   write   cut   read   drink

watch   sit   wear   play   cook   ride

drive

car – drive
bed – sleep
picture – draw
nose – smell
clothes – wear
chair – sit
ball – play
TV – watch
pot – cook
tea – drink
knife – cut
book – read
horse – ride
pencil – write

Miss Mouse is missing

Trage die entsprechenden Begriffe in das Rätselgitter ein,
und du erfährst, wo sich Miss Mouse versteckt hat!

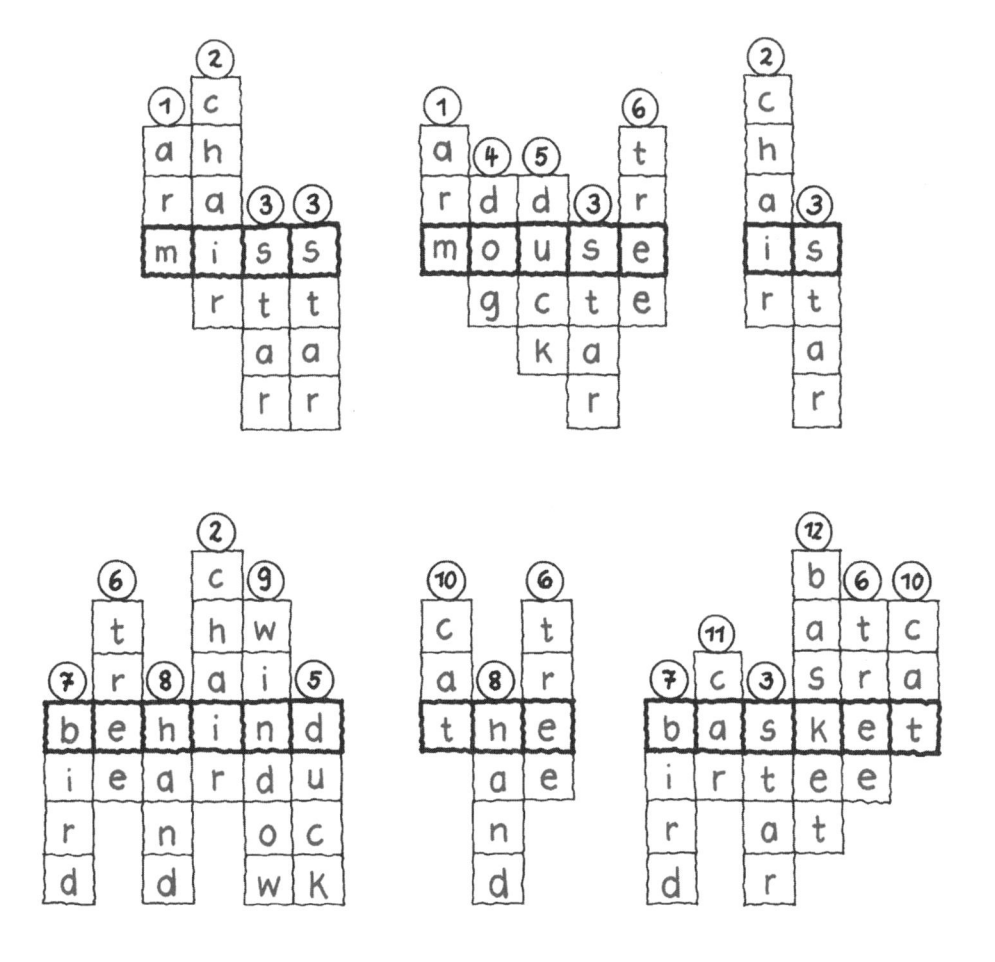

Rhyming pictures

Von 3 Bildern reimt sich jeweils eins nicht. Streiche es durch!

banana (box – fox)
candle (boot – foot)
apple (bee – tree)
cake (moon – spoon)
bucket (boat – coat)
bicycle (star – car)
knife (hat – cat)
telephone (pen – hen)
ruler (cake – lake)

Rhyming pictures

Von 3 Bildern reimt sich jeweils eins nicht. Streiche es durch!

house (frog – dog)
book (shirt – skirt)
cow (map – cap)
pencil (house – mouse)
car (clock – sock)
bed (sun – gun)
football (key – ski)
flower (eight – plate)
hand (rose – nose)

At school

Dieses Rätsel hat 2 Teile. „Übersetze" zuerst die Zahlen
in Buchstaben und schreibe sie darunter, z. B.:

9	5	2	6	4	11
c	a	r	p	e	t

Verbinde dann jedes Wort
mit dem passenden Bild!

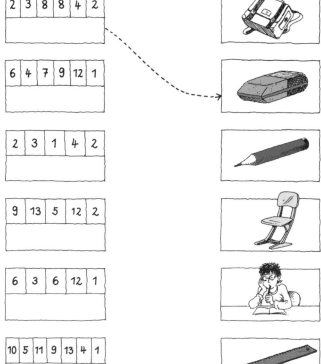

rubber
pencil
ruler
chair
pupil
satchel

Jobs

Schreibe den jeweiligen Beruf unter das passende Bild!
Die Silben im Kasten helfen dir dabei.

far-	nur-	ba-	but-	post-	-mer
pi-	tea-		cap-	-lot	-cher
-man	-se	-ker	-cher	-tain	

dentist

dentist
pilot
teacher
captain
farmer
postman
butcher
baker
nurse

A lot to see in our town

Lies die Wörter im unteren Kasten und male diejenigen Felder mit Rotstift aus,
in denen ein Begriff steht, den du im Bild sehen kannst.

Die ausgemalten Bilder ergeben
zusammen einen Buchstaben.
Welchen? Kreise ihn ein!

flag	ball	star	table	man
sun	girl	zebra	tree	egg
lemon	frog	boy	moon	cup
knife	house	flower	car	spoon
woman	basket	ship	banana	street

Im Bild:
flag
man
girl
tree
boy
house
car
woman
street

Lösung: x

New words

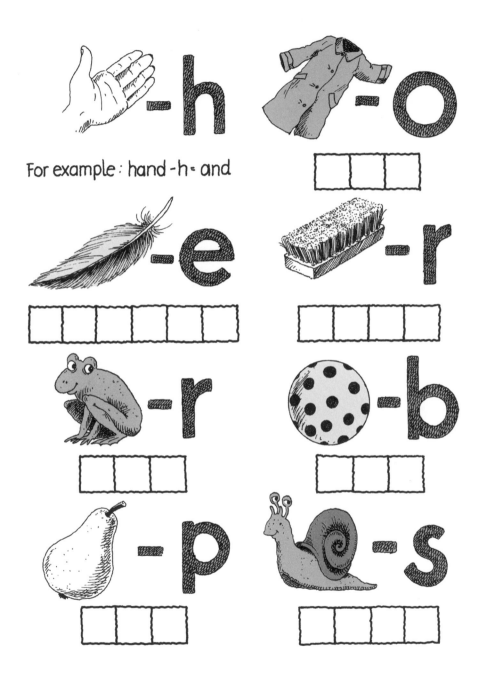

For example: hand -h = and

coat – o = cat
feather – e = father
brush – r = bush
frog – r = fog
ball – b = all
pear – p = ear
snail – s = nail

Numbers

Trage die ausgeschriebenen Zahlen in das Rätselgitter ein!

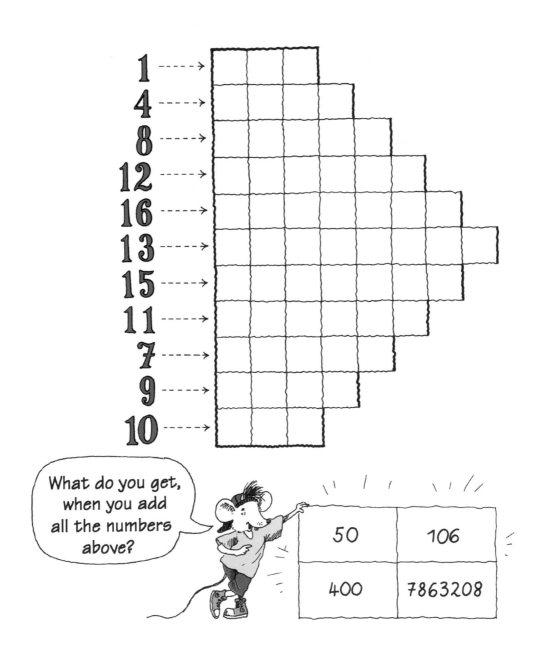

1 ----→
4 ----→
8 ----→
12 ----→
16 ----→
13 ----→
15 ----→
11 ----→
7 ----→
9 ----→
10 ----→

What do you get, when you add all the numbers above?

| 50 | 106 |
| 400 | 7863208 |

one
four
eight
twelve
sixteen
thirteen
fifteen
eleven
seven
nine
ten

If you add all the numbers,
you get 106.

Pictures and sentences

Schreibe in das Kästchen hinter jedem Satz den Erkennungsbuchstaben des dazugehörigen Bildes!

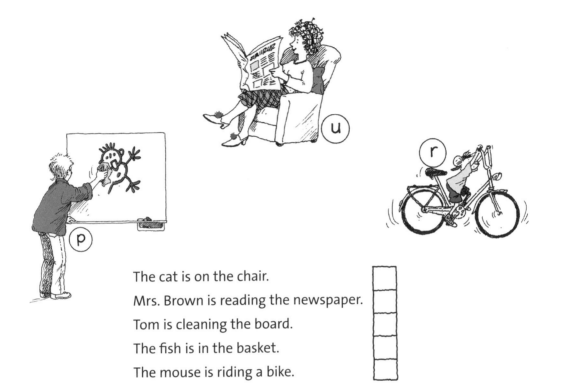

The cat is on the chair.

Mrs. Brown is reading the newspaper.

Tom is cleaning the board.

The fish is in the basket.

The mouse is riding a bike.

Lies die Lösungsbuchstaben von oben nach unten!

The cat is on the chair.

Mrs. Brown is reading the newspaper.

Tom is cleaning the board.

The fish is in the basket.

The mouse is riding a bike.

| S |
| U |
| P |
| E |
| R |

Pictures and sentences

Schreibe in das Kästchen hinter jedem Satz den Erkennungsbuchstaben des dazugehörigen Bildes!

The monkey is eating a banana.

Chris is reading a book.

Lucy goes shopping.

The children are laughing.

Bob is drawing a fish.

Lies die Lösungsbuchstaben von oben nach unten!

The monkey is eating a banana.

Chris is reading a book.

Lucy goes shopping.

The children are laughing.

Bob is drawing a fish.

| G |
| R |
| E |
| A |
| T |

Picture crossword

Trage den Namen jedes abgebildeten Gegenstands in das Kreuzworträtsel ein!

Wenn du die dick umrandeten Buchstaben hier einträgst, erhältst du das Lösungsmotto.
Aufgepasst: Die richtige Reihenfolge der Buchstaben musst du noch finden!

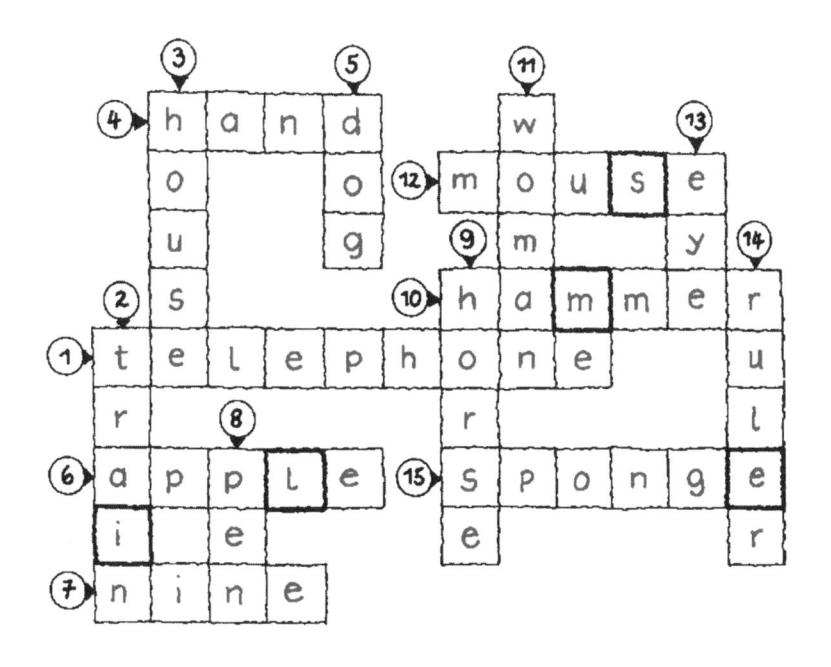

Lösung: smile!

Colours

Welche Farben haben die abgebildeten Dinge in Wirklichkeit?
Trage die Farben ins Rätselgitter ein!

			r	e	d		
	o	r	a	n	g	e	
	w	h	i	t	e		
	p	i	n	k			
			b	l	a	c	k
y	e	l	l	o	w		
	b	r	o	w	n		

Lösung: rainbow

Colours

Male die Felder in den angegebenen Farben aus! Drehe das
Bild um, wenn du fertig bist!

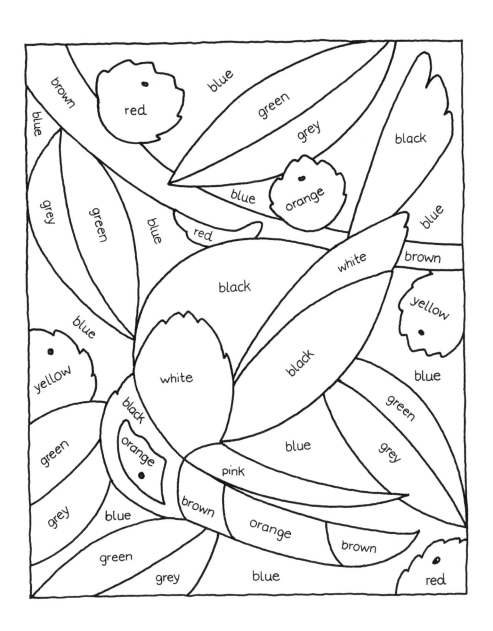

This bird is a toucan.

Complete the sentences!

Finde für jeden Satz die fehlende Präposition!

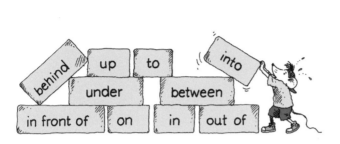

Miss Mouse is climbing _____ a ladder.

Miss Mouse is going _____ school.

Miss Mouse is sitting _____ a chair.

Miss Mouse is standing _____ two cats.

Miss Mouse is _____ a box.

Miss Mouse is playing _____ the garden.

Miss Mouse is looking _____ the tent.

Miss Mouse is going _____ the house.

Miss Mouse is reading _____ the table.

Miss Mouse is _____ the shop.

Miss Mouse is climbing up a ladder.
Miss Mouse is going to school.
Miss Mouse is sitting on a chair.
Miss Mouse is standing between two cats.
Miss Mouse is behind a box.
Miss Mouse is playing in the garden.
Miss Mouse is looking out of the tent.
Miss Mouse is going into the house.
Miss Mouse is reading under the table.
Miss Mouse is in front of the shop.

Hidden jobs...

Diese 9 Berufe findest du auch im Buchstabengitter. Kreise Sie mit einem Farbstift ein!
Achtung: Manche Buchstaben sind Bestandteil von 2 Wörtern.

c	e	n	i	f	v	d	t	r	a	m
a	n	r	a	k	d	e	m	i	e	f
p	o	s	t	m	a	n	e	t	v	a
t	b	p	i	l	o	t	n	e	d	r
a	a	r	l	a	m	i	l	a	h	m
i	k	o	n	u	r	s	e	c	h	e
n	e	m	o	b	u	t	c	h	e	r
a	r	h	e	d	o	f	r	e	n	k
n	d	l	a	n	w	i	t	r	l	e

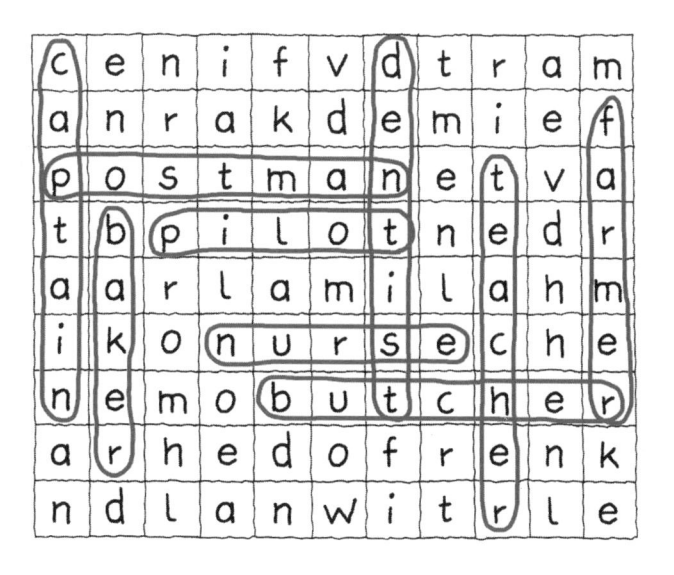

c	e	n	i	f	v	d	t	r	a	m
a	n	r	a	k	d	e	m	i	e	f
p	o	s	t	m	a	n	e	t	v	a
t	b	p	i	l	o	t	n	e	d	r
a	a	r	l	a	m	i	l	a	h	m
i	k	o	n	u	r	s	e	c	h	e
n	e	m	o	b	u	t	c	h	e	r
a	r	h	e	d	o	f	r	e	n	k
n	d	l	a	n	w	i	t	r	l	e

Hidden things...

Die 10 abgebildeten Dinge findest du auch im Buchstabengitter.
Kreise sie mit einem Farbstift ein!
Achtung: Manche Buchstaben sind Bestandteil von 2 Wörtern.

e	n	s	c	h	e	c	u	s	r
d	b	i	u	o	b	o	o	t	h
l	e	m	t	u	e	c	b	a	u
c	d	o	g	s	h	k	m	r	w
m	b	o	n	e	l	b	i	d	o
b	a	n	a	n	a	u	c	a	t
l	e	m	i	s	k	r	o	t	m
l	c	a	r	n	e	k	n	b	a

e	n	s	c	h	e	c	u	s	r
d	b	i	u	o	b	o	o	t	h
l	e	m	t	u	e	c	b	a	u
c	d	o	g	s	h	k	m	r	w
m	b	o	n	e	l	b	i	d	o
b	a	n	a	n	a	u	c	a	t
l	e	m	i	s	k	r	o	t	m
l	c	a	r	n	e	k	n	b	a

Things

Kennst du diese Dinge?
Schreibe Sie in das Rätselgitter!

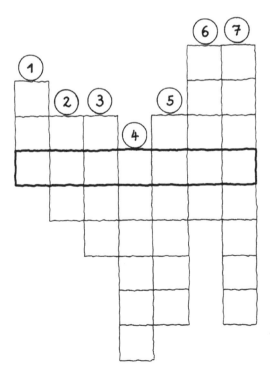

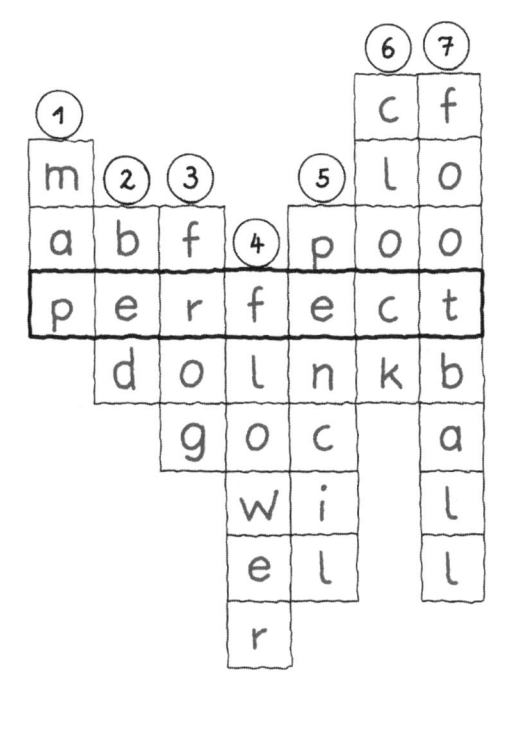